Douggie

the playful pup who became a
Sled Dog Hero

written by **PAM FLOWERS**

illustrated by **JON VAN ZYLE**

ALASKA
NORTHWEST
BOOKS®

From the beginning one puppy was different from the rest. He was big and black, his brother and sisters small and gray. While the others lay snuggled against their mother, this puppy wiggled constantly.

That pup's sure full of energy, thought Pam, the musher who owned the dogs.

Even before he could open his eyes, the black puppy learned to recognize Pam's scent and to love the gentle stroke of her hand.

Each day the puppies grew bigger. Soon their ears stood up, except the black pup's. His stayed flopped.

All day long he chased one puppy after another until he wore them all out. Then, while they slept, he chewed on their tails.

One morning Pam hunkered down close to the black puppy, who was tugging on his mother's tail. "I've got the perfect name for you," she said. "Douggie*, after Douglas Mawson, the famous Antarctic explorer. He was full of energy, too."

*"Douggie" is pronounced *dug -ē* (not *doog -gē*).

When the puppies were three months old, Pam showed them a small, red harness. First, she put it on Roald, Douggie's brother, who looked proud and confident. The other pups crowded around, eager to try it on next.

When Pam slipped the harness over Douggie's head he wiggled with excitement. In a flash he grabbed the strap between his teeth, jerked his head up, and flipped himself clean over.

Pam sighed. "We'll try again later."

To celebrate their six-month birthdays, Pam let the puppies try out for her team. Instead of pulling the sled, Douggie ran along barking in Roald's ear trying to get him to play.

Douggie was the only pup who didn't make the team.

The next winter, he tried again. This time he got so excited he chewed through the towline setting free the dogs in front of him.

As the sled lurched to a halt, the loose dogs disappeared around a bend. Pam scowled. "If you don't learn to calm down, Douggie, you'll *never* make this team."

Each year when the team left on a trek, Douggie stayed behind.

But he didn't give up. He practiced every day pulling a toy sled loaded with firewood back and forth over the trail. Slowly Douggie improved.

Meanwhile, Pam planned her next expedition: a dangerous 325-mile trek to the Magnetic North Pole with Roald as lead dog.

Pam hoped Douggie could come, but she was worried. Douggie was already three years old and had failed to make the team twice. *I'll give him one more chance,* she thought. *If he doesn't make it, I can't waste any more time working with him.*

But during that year's tryouts, Douggie amazed Pam. He started following her commands, showing he knew "Gee" meant turn right, "Haw" meant turn left, "Whoah" meant stop, and "Let's go" meant start.

This time, Douggie made the team!

In fact, he did so well over the next few months that Pam made a surprising decision.

"Douggie, you're going to be my number two lead dog, next to Roald," she said.

Douggie wiggled with excitement.

Then late one night, something terrible happened. A moose walked into the dog lot and kicked Roald, injuring him badly.

No one felt like training without Roald. The dogs lay curled up in their houses and Pam sat in her cabin crying. "Should I cancel the expedition?" she wondered.

But the next day Douggie was pacing around like he wanted to get back to work. Pam smiled. "You're right, Douggie. Time to start training again." As soon as she touched the sled, every dog sprang to its feet, raring to go.

"Douggie, you're my new lead dog," said Pam. "If we're going to make it to the Magnetic North Pole, we'll need your energy."

The day they started on their long journey, the weather turned very cold. But the dogs, Douggie, Matt, and Robert, in their thick fur coats and Pam in her heavy parka stayed warm.

They were happy traveling together. The land around them was silent except for the dogs' light panting and the constant rasp of the sled runners over the snow. There were no trees, no people, just the barren white beauty of the sea ice they were crossing.

Soon they settled into a comfortable routine. Each morning Pam and the dogs rose early and devoured a big breakfast before setting out. Lunch was doggy pizza—water-soaked food frozen into flat slabs. The dogs loved the *crunch, crunch, crunch* it made as they gobbled it down.

Most days were enjoyable, but stormy weather was no fun. As the wind rose, Pam quickly made shelters by turning the sleds on their sides. Snow swirled around them and wind roared through camp. As the dogs huddled together waiting out the storm, Pam listened to the *craaack* of the sea ice shifting all around them.

During those storms, powerful
winds shoved the sea ice so hard that
huge pieces broke off. Thick slabs of ice
pushed against one another, thrusting higher
and higher until they formed jagged mountains.

As lead dog, Douggie had to guide them through this
confusing maze. Watching Douggie concentrate, Pam felt proud.
She could hardly believe this was the same wiggly puppy that had been
too excited to make the team.

Day after day they trudged through the ice, slipping, often falling, but Douggie always kept them going. His energy never ran out.

But when they came to ice piled as high as a house, the expedition ground to a halt. They were still many days' away from the Magnetic North Pole. Pam worried. What if they got stuck and ran out of food? They could die.

Maybe it's time to go home, she thought.

But Douggie wasn't ready to quit. He gave the sleds a mighty tug.

"Okay, Douggie," Pam nodded. "If you're willing to try, so are we."

As the dogs struggled through more rough ice, Douggie suddenly stopped and jerked his nose toward the sky, sniffing nervously. A movement off to the right caught Pam's eye.

POLAR BEAR!

It was lurking behind a pile of ice, silently watching them. Pam could see blood on its shoulder. She did not want to tangle with a wounded bear.

"Douggie, let's go," Pam called softly.

He inched forward. But when he came to the bear's tracks Douggie stopped. The strange scent excited him. He swung right, following the tracks.

Douggie was heading straight for the polar bear!

H aw, Douggie!" yelled Pam.

But Douggie didn't stop. It was as though he couldn't even hear her.

As they drew closer and closer, the bear raised its mighty paw, ready to strike.

Terrified, Pam screamed again, "Douglas! Haw!"

Startled by Pam's tone, Douggie finally heard her. Suddenly realizing their danger, he jerked away from the bear and raced the team across the ice.

"Is it chasing us?" Pam cried, but she didn't look back.

Eventually, Douggie stopped. Trembling and breathing in ragged gasps, Pam looked over her shoulder. The bear was gone.

THEY WERE SAFE.

From then on, Douggie always followed Pam's commands. He still had enough energy for three dogs, but he never let his excitement take over again.

After nineteen days of difficult travel, Douggie led the team past the last pile of ice and charged onto a beautiful, flat, snow-covered beach. Free of the ice, Douggie ran flat out until everyone was gasping for breath. When they finally stopped, Pam checked her map.

"We made it!" she shouted, throwing her hands in the air.

"THE MAGNETIC NORTH POLE!"

When Pam dug into her sled bag and pulled out three steaks, all three dogs wiggled for joy. The biggest steak went to Douggie.

Pam kneeled beside Douggie and gently stroked his back. "You did it, Douggie! You came through every time we needed you. Without your energy we never would have made it."

Douggie wiggled and barked and wagged his tail furiously. Pam laughed and for once she didn't try to calm him down.

EPILOGUE

On April 9, 1991, Pam and her three dogs set out alone from Resolute Bay, Canada, to mush 325 miles to the Magnetic North Pole. Traveling only by surface over the traditional route used by previous explorers, they reached their goal on April 27, 1991. The team survived many challenges and returned home safely and in good spirits.

A few years later, Douggie set out on another exciting adventure. Along with Anna, a young inexperienced number two lead dog, Douggie led Pam and a team of eight dogs 2,500 miles across the Arctic. You can read about that expedition in *Big-Enough Anna* and *Alone Across the Arctic*, by Pam Flowers with Ann Dixon (Alaska Northwest Books).

To my friend Alice Holinger, who is always
ready to give someone another chance.

—P. F.

For all the good leaders I've had
throughout my years of mushing.

—J. V. Z.

Text © 2008 by Pam Flowers
Illustrations © 2008 by Jon Van Zyle

LSI

Library of Congress Cataloging-in-Publication Data
Flowers, Pam.
   Douggie : the playful pup who became a sled dog hero /
written by Pam Flowers ; illustrated by Jon Van Zyle.
     p. cm.
   ISBN 978-0-88240-654-1 (hardbound)
   ISBN 978-0-88240-655-8 (softbound)
1. Sled dogs—Alaska—Juvenile literature. 2.
Dogsledding—Alaska—Juvenile literature. 3.
Dogsledding—Arctic regions—Juvenile literature. 4.
Flowers, Pam—Travel—Arctic regions—Juvenile
literature. I. Van Zyle, Jon. II. Title.

   SF428.7.F5925 2007
   636.73—dc22

                    2007023555

Editor: Michelle McCann
Design: Elizabeth Watson and Jon Van Zyle
Mapmaker: Gray Mouse Graphics

Published byAlaska Northwest Books®
an imprint of

WEST
MARGIN
PRESS
WestMarginPress.com

Proudly distributed by Ingram Publisher Services

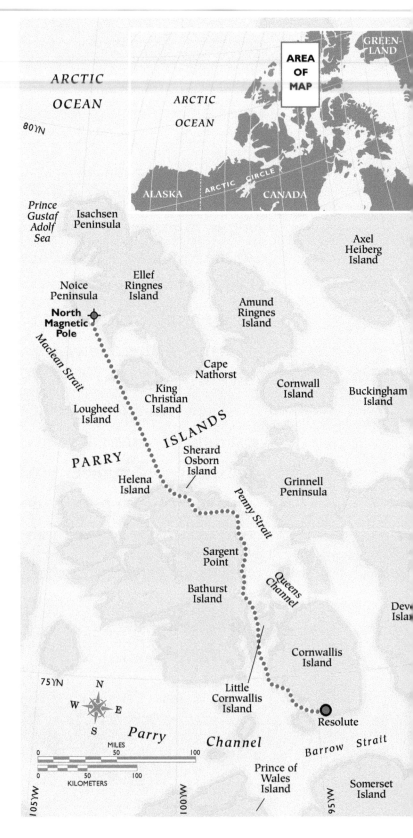

Printed in the USA
CPSIA information can be obtained
at www.ICGtesting.com
JSHW070801121223
53613JS00034B/189